LATE IN THE EMPIRE OF MEN

LATE IN THE
EMPIRE OF MEN

CHRISTOPHER KEMPF

Four Way Books
Tribeca

Please direct all inquiries to:
Editorial Office
Four Way Books
POB 535, Village Station
New York, NY 10014
www.fourwaybooks.com

Library of Congress Cataloging-in-Publication Data

Names: Kempf, Christopher, author.
Title: Late in the empire of men / Christopher Kempf.
Description: New York, NY : Four Way Books, 2017.
Identifiers: LCCN 2016034899 | ISBN 9781935536871 (pbk. : alk. paper)
Classification: LCC PS3611.E5327 A6 2017 | DDC 811/.6--dc23
LC record available at https://lccn.loc.gov/2016034899

Funding for this book was provided in part by a generous donation in memory of John J. Wilson.

We are a proud member of the Community of Literary Magazines and Presses.

Distributed by University Press of New England
One Court Street, Lebanon, NH 03766

for my parents, who taught me to read

Contents

"I think that a day will come when the names of Denver and Sioux City will have a traditional and antique dignity like Damascus and Perugia—and when it will not seem grotesque to us that it is so."
　　—Van Wyck Brooks, *The Wine of the Puritans*

"Imperialism, of which petrifacts such as the Egyptian empire, the Roman, the Chinese, the Indian may continue to exist for hundreds or thousands of years—dead bodies, amorphous and dispirited masses of men, scrap-material from a great history—is to be taken as the typical symbol of the passing away. Imperialism is Civilization unadulterated. In this phenomenal form the destiny of the West is now irrevocably set."
　　—Oswald Spengler, *The Decline of the West*

Sledding at Harding Memorial

It was how humans, the future will say,
entertained themselves those last centuries
winter existed. Cribs of dogwood racked
in the side yard. Jarred fruit. Fat
in our snowsuits, my sister & I approached
together the gate's wrought bars. Beyond them
the President, we understood, slept
beside his wife in the frozen, stone-set earth
of Ohio. Here, in 1923, street
after street of our hometown trimmed
in black felt, his funeral train paraded
at last to a stop. The body, blocked
in ice since California, face wired shut, sunk
slowly in its chamber, & later that evening
the team of men whose job it was rose
from their dinners & lifted into place
the great slab, something paleolithic laid
at the spot where history limped away
to remember itself. & somewhere far
below us our father watched. I held my sister
in my legs & allowed, as he'd done, the numbed
earth to pull us toward him. Wind
lashed our faces. The formed plastic
of the sled scored the ground behind us, & after
we had stopped, our father, become
suddenly a beast in harness, hauled us

back. Like that, Spengler says,
the pyramids rose—ranks of men
bent forward, the future's certain devastations
arrested by inscripted stone. & roping
our sled to his own he towed us, colorful
train of blood & plastic, back,
then, to the hill's edge, & together, pressed
tight against disaster, that very last
of our grand tombs looming above us, we began
again the descent.

Information Age

Those weekends, while Bradleys gathered
on Kuwait's northern border—their barrels
raised, the tankers'
breath drawn—our father,
on the kitchen table, arranged
the hulking Macintosh he'd brought home
in his Chrysler Horizon. Five

that year, as yet
unlettered in the epic ensuing
beyond our block, I watched with my sister
the flickering disk drive light
its small beacon beneath
his touch. The dull screen
shimmered to life. Like

this, he'd say taking
our hands in his own & holding
our fingers to the keys. & we, first
in terror then
in awe watched
the strange combinations of letters rend
the darkness. DOS. The chalky
cursor. The whir
& clicking the disk drive, like
a man, moved
through its work with. When,

in *fin de siècle* Boston, Bell
to the mouthpiece plucked
an electrical reed, he
heard first the same mechanical static. He flattened
his ear to the signal's hissing, as if,
there in his basement, hailed
by some inscrutable future. Our father

huddled before the screen. Oh *son*
et lumière machine. Oh we
who in that new light looked
like a family folding
in on itself on the shores
of a burning empire. On the Tigris,

tanks in formation. In the basement, Bell
to Watson—do you follow
what I am telling you? Yes,
he said. We entered
our names & erased them.

Call of Duty: Modern Warfare

For which my brother huddled
all night in the lot of some box
    store on Coliseum. & the pealing

guns of which split
the walls of our bedroom for months, much
    like Baghdad I imagined,

whose fathers bomb-
proofed the ears of their children each night
    at bedtime. Except,

you know, not. Not
the wrecked roof & welts
    where the metal held them.

Not the smart bomb & boxes
of dead. The ex-box. The X-
    marks-the-spot box. Not

the wedge of flag our neighbor
David came back as. That
    night we fired

round after round at brown-
skinned, scarf-fitted pixels. In
    high-resolution, the wound

blooming like a kiss. Call
of Duty—the digital,
    Middle Eastern teenager toppling. Want

is rarely respectable. What
this century left us is just
    this one way to be men. If x,

then why? When the sky
explodes, strap on
    your body.

Lacrimae rerum

tears for things

As for empathy, it was breakfast
that taught me first the feelings
    of objects. Each

wet Cheerio floated there despairing,
it seemed, to be—bare
    raft—wrenched

like that from its family. Food
was just the beginning. I pitied
    the drooping head of the desk lamp, the light

bulb its burning out. I endowed
with the pathos of selfhood whole
    herds of stuffed beasts—Bianca

the platypus, Paul the goat. Baudelaire,
in a late essay, contends the child's finding
    of a soul in her playthings exhibits

what he terms the earliest
metaphysical tendency. How shameful
    it seemed, that we—who had,

after all, imagined these things & made them
in our image—endured
    with our lives while, for them, the death

of all exhausted commodities
awaited. Or worse. I remember
    understanding that crayons

as they colored consumed
themselves. That shoes, shuffling
    even casually about their business, disintegrated

slowly. Son
of Anchises, Aeneas knew too the tears
    to be shed for objects. He watched

in terror Troy, in a Carthaginian mural, burned
to the ground again, wept
    there for his countrymen, yes, but also,

Virgil explains, for the banquet
of golds & pinks the painter
    fed to the ruins. *Sunt*

lacrimae rerum. Rome,
he meant, was itself constructed
    from weeping. Once,

in a different century, my own father
brought back from his wandering
    across the sea a small

Continental jet plane. Its main
retracting wheels rose,
        with a satisfying click, inside it. The tips

of its hinged wings lifted. & when,
one summer, it vanished
        in the move, I knew then

this was how it would go for us. That suffered
to its logical end empathy
        implied, as life did, a dying

of the self into something outside it. South
of Malaysia this morning, men
        are searching the water

for wreckage. An engine
perhaps. A seat. Some
        kind of consoling object to hold

their sadness. Some black
box chock-
        full of it.

The Indianapolis 500

"Mike Conway injures left leg in airborne crash"
—*The Indianapolis Star*, May 30, 2010

This also we took
            from the gods. Robbed
                        fire & driveshaft & strapped
    both to the back of a man more
                        bird now than human. How,
        in Ovid, they look on,
those deities, indifferently
        at Icarus slipping from the sky. How seas
                        open. The whine

    of Hondas drowns even
                        this place's cicadas. It's something
Roman almost.
        Like aqueduct. Like dome. Roman
                        our wanting just this
        exact catastrophe to happen. Our wanting
    to watch. A man,

                        after all, enters
myth only so many ways this century. Proficiency
        at killing things is one. Another
                        is upcycling his six-
    cylinder in the middle
                        of turn four, the fans
    there knowing already it will end

in mangled carbon fiber & flame. In the weightless
                    cicada shell of his car cutting
        across the sky like a discus. Icarus

    knew well the way
                we learn violence is by trying
                            to fly & falling. Who felt
the sky draw back like a lover
            above its floodgates & drank
                            the sea instead. The sons
    of this place plummet, of course, to concrete
        eventually. They are shredded
                            & smoke. They stagger
    away mostly, those
                among us who up
                            from all that wreckage
        walk.

Predictive Text: The Corn Monster

It was our father
who taught us. He watched us,
                                    the monster, from deep
    in the field's whisper. We'd listen
                    to its dry scraping & wait,
                                        but it too moved
    when we moved & moved
                with much rustling like something
    impossibly larger than us. It mumbled
                                    in a raspy accent we had
no answer for. My phone,

    when I remember & text
                                    my sister this, suggests
            instead *the born monster* & aren't
we all? Often
                                        it will do this, predict
    cool when I mean to say *book* & *good*
                when I want to say *home*, imposing
                            its own semantics like a man
who has been out drinking & says *this*
        is the way it will be now
                                my little ones. & when,

        one summer, the cows escaped, I said
                            the cows have escaped & stood
    with my sister squinching

our faces to the glass. The dads
of our street's three families fashioned
                              broomsticks into prods & stalked
        together into the darkness. They marched
in their loose circle herding
                the cattle like matadors, their dance the dance
                                        of all art, of man
        & animal & of the single steer
we heard screaming from the field. There was one

                gunshot & our father, taller
    now than he would ever be, buckling
                              the stalks. There was talk
        of mercy & mud, something
we could barely hear as he wiped his hands
                                        & made his way
    across the yard toward our good home,
            toward my sister & I, Amy, whose name
                          means *love*, but comes up now
    as *boy* & *box* & *cow*.

Oregon Trail

Before I was a man I was a man
made of pixels, a glittering
column of dots drawn
west across the earth by word
of land limitless & given freely
to him who worked it. First,
on the line assigned, I typed
the names of my children, fitted
our wagon with axle grease & for each
child a change of clothing. I followed
the pathway day
by day across Nebraska, my rations
set to *filling*, my four
head of oxen walking
steady. Spirits
were high. *To hunt,*
the instructions said, *enter*
'BANG' as quickly as possible. I slaughtered,
with my deft spelling, elk
& buffalo, whole
herds of antelope & my family
sucked on the bones til Bridger. Beyond
our school's computer lab that month,
Yousef's Ryder truck erupted
in a parking garage somewhere
we had never heard of, its twenty-foot

16

fuse looping cartoon-like,
I imagined, to the packed
bed. Back
in 1855, miners
with the Lupton party charged
at sunrise a tribe of Takelma camping
near the trail. They tore
women from their husbands, from
the arms of their mothers cut
the little ones & ran them through
Bowie-knife spine to hilt. *To hunt,*
the instructions said, *enter.* We bent
our faces to the screen, keyed
the letters again
& again & let
the meat of the pronghorn rot
in our wagons. We contracted
typhoid, forded
the river at the South Pass & were dragged
in the mad flux under. *Amy
has drowned. Dad
has measles.* We marched
with our diseases seaward & wrote—when at last
we succumbed to snakebite, our tiny
pixels flickering in the dusk somewhere
at the edge of the West—wrote

there our own
epitaphs on the line provided. Behind us
on the map our path
wound like a fuse across the continent. *Congratulations,*
the game said. *Press*
SPACE to continue.

In the '90s

In the '90s we were five. We were pirates
each Halloween & wore our teeth
   black like the blacked-out

windows of the cities we were bombing. We watched
each night the neon tracers blaze
   the sky of our televisions, listened

to Peter Jennings, who was Canadian,
explain it—how Baghdad
   was a real city somewhere though it sounded

like a sackful of fathers. How the mosques
wailed for days. We didn't know,
   in the '90s, we were poor. We played

with army men in the desert
of our dingy living room floor, with Legos
   on the ocean of our bedrooms. We moved

twice in the '90s. We liked Mike. We liked
90210 & soaps. We didn't know
   what sex was in the '90s

then we knew. We named
an 80-acre mall for our country. The cops
   clubbed Rodney King on camera

in the '90s, we saw it. We watched
all night in the '90s the night
   Diana died. We cried. We cried

many times in the '90s. In the '90s
we turned 15. In the '90s
   we wore JNCO jeans & believed

in aliens & the Hale-Bopp comet. We got
our first erections in the '90s & knew then
   to stand several inches from Katie Harel

while "All My Life" played slowly
in the morbid cafetorium. We combined
   words in the '90s & this saved us

a few dollars. In the '90s
we invented the internet. We spent
   hours while the modem groaned

its horrible foreign language like the world
was about to end. The world
   was always about to end

in the '90s. One night—
this was the '90s—we dressed in all black. We packed
   our bags with toilet paper & draped

the Hass sisters' sycamores
in white. & every one of us,
    that night, watched the ribbons

lifted into the darkness, & the sky
of the '90s—it took what we gave it & waving
    above us its hundred

white flags flung
back, in the '90s, its salvo
    of used-up tubes.

Blackout, 2003

In the photograph afterward,
                                    a fake, the field
            of darkness exists simply
as backlit absence. Elsewhere
                        the highways blaze—Las Vegas
            & San Francisco some glittering,
                                                intricately
connected galaxy. & that

            was what we saw that weekend,
                                    wasn't it? Above us
        the pale band of the Milky Way wheeling
                                into motion again. Neptune
            flashing. Packed

in a dorm room east of Cleveland we,
            who had just that week arrived & by candlelight
                        had abandoned our parents, passed
        among us a dozen
                            or so stale tallboys. Our billowing
shadows moved on the cinderblock walls. Small
                            tongues of flame shaped
themselves again
            & again & it seemed to us, drunk
                                    there, we existed
            at last at the beginning
of some great & promising culture. Cut

loose from progress. Long

      before Dutch colonists bought Manhattan
for a necklace, the Lenape watched
                            each evening these
    same forgotten constellations arrange
            themselves in the heavens. History
    followed. Smallpox
              & light. Salvation,

Benjamin writes, requires
                just the tiniest of fissures
    in enlightenment. In Ohio

            that weekend, workers
      in plastic buckets climbed night
& day across the faulty substation the bug
           began at. Appliances
    flickered with life.
                    On the horizon

our college's Gothic arches, dark
        vaults of brick, lifted
                back the galaxy

   that had astonished us once. We crushed
the empties in on themselves. Outside

the night shone. Its so much

light we called it

                  pollution. We knew

then we'd be sick with it.

Bindery

Nights that semester, the rest
of campus deep in its Baroque paintings

& trig functions above me, I milled
the spines from a stack of back issues. I slid

the loose ream to Mike, a man
who for half a century had stood

at a bench in the library's basement binding
the separate issues into one. The industrial-

gauge needle dropped & retracted, his stack
of acid-free paper punctured

beneath it. This, he said once, requires
of us the most devoted of care. I covered

the stacks with adhesive & sheathed them
in marbleized backing. We bound

the back issues exactly
& in silence, Mike

& I, while
on a TV in the corner the war worked

its way at last to the National
Museum of Iraq. We watched

together the vast catalog of loss. Lyres
of Ur, oldest

of stringed instruments. The earliest
mask of the face in fragments. I passed

the sewn-up, coverless book back
to Mike who mounted the bare ream

in its buckram cover—classics
in red, economics indigo. History,

on the late news, loosed
itself again into bedlam. Men

fled the museum heaped
with Sumerian jewelry. They moved

silently, guided
by the lights of choppers

in the sky above them, by
the burning oil fields the future

to which we were bound
would be lit with.

Clearing the History

Then it was finished.
                    Whimper.
                                   Bang.
             I clicked. I pictured
   beneath me my afternoon's study—well-hung
                         deliverymen tendering their mouths
to the crotches of housewives, webcam
                              punk girls—swirling
      & tumbling in the hard drive's
                              drain hole. Below
our cornfields real
            amateurs, I imagined, merged
with our neighbors' filth, flowing, the whole
                              sweet concoction, out
        toward some distant ocean. We know,

   now, there is no such architecture. That every
                              keystroke, every
          twelve-girl gang bang is cached
to a government server somewhere
                    in the desert in a basement
                         even the fault lines, its designers
        say, will not disturb. I wanted,

           though, when I came to California, to forget
my father in the doorway. The way

he did not hit me. Did not
for a single instant acknowledge
                                the blonde, unbelievably
            limber babysitter fist-
    fucking on his office computer, or later, lowering
his eyes in shame, my first girlfriend
                        as she vaulted the couch. I wanted, yes,

to forget his sexless marriage, my parents'
                            slow dying together
        in Ohio. Also
its winters. Its working class clocking in
            to swing shifts at Marion Steel. Stadiums
                            of howling men letting out
their rage on some small tribe
            of boys dressed in the brightest of armor. It is true

                        there is not a single cemetery
    still used in San Francisco. The summer
                            I arrived, I roamed
        the Tenderloin's sex clubs until I was one
with the throbbing city. I sunned myself
            on its glossy beaches, above which
                        guns from the last war, massive
long-abandoned batteries, chaperoned
                        Chinese cargo tankers sailing in
        through the vital gate.

29

Gun

                go bang bang. One

        will note, of course, the sex
     that leaked from everything. The suggestion,
       also, it is never really cleared,
                  history, that it
  is carried inside us like a seed,
         though wasn't California, field
   of gold, that so much
           newness we had longed for? Forget
  how it ended—
             I spent my savings. I became
my father. When the Spanish saw it

          it brought them to their knees.

Dominion

"& God said unto them, Be fruitful, & multiply, & replenish the
earth, & subdue it: & have dominion over the fish of the sea, &
over the fowl of the air, & over every living thing that moveth
upon the earth."
—Genesis 1:28

But to the trees we are,
like metaphor, mostly

extraneous, our language,
to them, the breath-

play of peasants. Picture
this world without us,

you say, the sick planet picked
clean—as by a kind

of divine wind—of ruin
& war. Of word. We turn

west on the Redwood Trail late
on a Sunday. The endangered

sequoias vanish above us
& there is nothing, you say,

or no place the planet
is unaffected. Its feverish

heaving. The breathing trees turning
over & over their old

air. We are
all of us lung. What

Cabrillo breathed. What bands
of Ohlone women walked

beside in silence. I
would be for you

like the railroad the ravager
of all of this. Would give

vast acreages to make you
immortal. I am not

in the slightest sorry. Tonight
I will tie you to the bed—bolted

pinewood—& we
will make the frame whine. & when

the idea of people
is over, as I hope

it is quickly, I hope
the trees remain. The language-

less. In-
describable night.

Shady Cove

This far downriver the rapids,
the maps explain, are not what they are
in Eagle Point. Or Prospect
even, or Agness, though still
the current can, like a whip, reach
out & take a boy. One knows
this living here. One
has heard of Nicholas Reardon. Of rock
& bone. One knows
too, however, the water
is deep in places & cool & the town
is small. The six boys, blue-
lipped at the river's edge, eye
beneath them the tensed sheet
of the Rogue. They know
the girls who are watching them expect
from them something astounding
& line up one
after another to plummet
from the great cliffs. It
is the dead center of summer. The cicadas'
ancient love song throbs
in the shade trees. The town—tired
backwater capital,
with its progress, forgot—gathers
in on itself shirking
the heat. & I, lost here

on my way to a city the six of them
will never, it is likely, buy
their girlfriends dinner in or watch reflect
from its million panes of glass the last
light of day, drink
beer on the boat launch & watch
their shimmering bodies, buoy-
like, rise. How slightly, notice,
the poem has drifted here
into myth. Icarus
climbing from the labyrinth, etc. Six
boys on the edge of manhood. They hurl
their bodies to the water, I want
to say, the way
they will, in a decade, take
at seventy the bend on Hammell Road. One
understands there is a logic
the economy of a small town tends
toward. War
& wreckage. One
of the boys, emboldened
perhaps by the gathering evening, approaches
at last a lingering girl. It begins—
the myth of love—once
again in Shady Cove. He knows
this time it will be different.
He is shivering.

Gold Star Tree

From somewhere in its Pennsylvania field, felled
there by a man who had all his life
        laid the thing's wind-damaged branches
                        in splints, who in
    the spring of each year cleared free
the small boughs, he
        explains now to the cameras, we call
                        candles—a man
    that is, who for just this moment
had raised it—the great
                twenty-foot fir arrives. A row

    of Marines wheels into position
                       & lifts, & later
tonight we will all of us watch—ribbons
     of bronze bunched into flowers, filigreed
                  snowflakes. David

    Sanchez, your name
is on a star in the President's living room. You,
        who in our school's cafeteria appeared
             one day dressed
  in the dress-blue uniform war
    is made handsome with & one day
swallowed the Tigris. The tank's—

                                        they said—tin-
                    can inside filling
with water. & when

            I shall die, Juliet prays, take him
        & cut him out in little stars & he,
                            she says, will make
            the face of the heavens blush. Beauty,
                        she means, is the cruelest kind
        of dying. David

        are you lonely in Andromeda? Are you watching,
    even now, our new constellations arranging
                        themselves in Firdos Square? That sheer,
                            chiffon-like fog
                of nebulae gathering
                            in Baghdad. David
    who by RPG & IED. David
                        who by crash & car bomb. Who by
        such small-arms fire fell. Your family,

                        when they visit, can print
        the date of your death, David,
    on your metal star & sometimes,
                        perhaps, the President,

on his way to the kitchen, will lift
his face to your radiance—raised
    as you have been, David, in the boughs
                        of the state—& consider, O star
                                of wonder, star
of glory & blood, your brightest
    trajectory. Westward

                        leading, David. Still

    proceeding.

What Happens in Vegas

is almost invisible in the glitter. City
from the sky like a rhinestone. Or see,
    rather, what once

the Spanish saw—spread
of green fields fed
    by well. What

the earliest evangelists named *vegas*. Staging
point. Promise
    of water. Where,

instead, the West lapped back
on itself like a flood
    & festered. Spread

legs of the Empire Club. Front
of the Mirage, a man
    dressed as SpongeBob beats

the pavement. Off
Paradise a warehouse heaped
    with meat. With sweet-

bread. With stomach & tongue. Touch
nothing. Or touch
    only the lapped mouth money

can buy. *I*—one
hooker to another—*have been working*
    all month on my moan. Oh,

Vegas. The lake
of your Bellagio—*beautiful*
    almost—explodes every hour

to the music of Cher, the same
water, rumor
    has it, the city

showers with. Consider
that moment. To hose
    from one's skin six

times per shift the salt
of men. Remember
    that like the flesh faith

is peddled easily here & belief
is our dearest myth. Let history
    be banished to the desert. Let the rest

of the city drink, now,
from its own mouth
    & be drunk.

Okay, Cupid

I admire you most, boldly
drawn boy in Bronzino's
   Venus. Oil on wood. Where you,

Cupid, cup
your mother's breast & bend
   your pale, putto's mouth to hers. How

disturbed they were
in Florence by your bit
   of incest, as if

by your hips, by your thrust buttocks, Love
itself had been abandoned. Man
   & god. Not

the doe-eyed child valentines
swoon to, you
   know best the pleasure of the packed

fist, the full,
wrist-deep dark. Drive
   hard, the heart is planted deep. Draw

your bent bow. So
do I love, under-
   stand. Self-

summary—what I did
in the locked stall of the Chevron station made me
    sick. Still,

what I want is
not Botticelli. Instead,
    that any moment might,

like Christ—or like
you, Cupid—become,
    suddenly, flesh. The fitness

center. The city
bus, or bakery. Make
    the long loaves rise. I

am looking for—the throat hold, the hips
pinned to the mattress, & after
    we have exhausted the present tense to let

my body fall
apart from some other's sucking
    air. There

is a time for tenderness, yet
there is also the bite mark's mouth. Maimed
    skin. Six

things I could never do without—how
many holes does a body have? Here,
    Cupid, you came

to earth girdled in shame. You showed
the rest of us love
    is plural. Pull

to your ear the arrow's
fletchery. Message
    me if—

Venice Beach

All along the boardwalk
    today the smog
is moving in the slogan shirts. TWERK,
    et cetera. Solomon
the Fortune Teller shells pistachios
    & asks me for the time. I tell him
it is the off season. Our beach
    is abandoned. A man,

I read last week, ramped
    the curb here in his Dodge Avenger then,
drunk probably, launched
    the car toward the weekend's peak
crowd, killing one. The blood,
    the tabloids said, scrubbed out—absent
rainfall—finally
    only with jackhammers. Here,

though, I am just beginning
    to tan. The sand
is warm. I am watching
    a pair of nearly perfect brunettes flex
& pose for each other, one
    girl holding the iPhone while the other,
her friend, chest
    heaving, hair

wet on her shoulders, rolls
    in the pounding surf. Their swimsuits
glisten. As if
    they are giving off sound, they square
their phones to their bodies, beautiful
    now as they will ever be
& careless. America,

    I am older & sadder. I remember
your mothers, America, carrying
    your children to the mall & making them
radiant. Bangs
    like the rolling tide. Rhinestone.
We shined, it seemed, with such
    a classic resplendence then
remember? In Venice

    the girls' bodies are talking
to their phones in a language long
    beyond my own understanding now. They bow
for the tiny camera. They capture
    each other arranging
themselves like statues
    in the dark waves, most ancient
of Death's symbols. I am thinking

of Arnold for instance. Who glimpsed
in the evening tide the turbid flow
    of human misery & who,
when God had died, decided
    we must become ourselves
that sweetness. The three of us,
    one in that work, watch
together the ebbing surf. *Turbid,*

    he called it, a word
we have in Venice essentially
    forgotten but which, in that century, meant
a kind of murkiness. The churned-up
    dust & sand obscuring
the water. We can see it
    this evening in each
ascending scroll. So
    also we called the waves once.

Sutro Baths

San Francisco, 2014

What remains is wasted rock. Runes
of some gang's spray-
    painted graffiti. The sea's

scud. Sometime,
however, by the end
    of the 19th century, men

had mastered at last the magic
of carburized iron. Light enough,
    that new metal, to stretch,

shimmering, far above
their dozen acres of ocean. & so inside
    the Pacific the city swam. & such

turbines there were, & slides,
six of them, & springboards. Electric
    pumps. In Pompeii,

we know, whole networks
of ducts & conduits brought
    to each city block its washing

fountain. Pools
of salt water & fresh. By flushing
    plaster in, they are able,

archaeologists, to haul
from the earth exact casts
   of the disaster—a dog

on its chain raising
its paws to its face, a family
   of four folded

in each other's arms, the feet
of the youngest positioned
   on her father's shoulders. We know

from graffiti the family's
name. *Petellius.* Elsewhere
   in the city—*Aufidius*

was here. Here
I made bread. Already
   in these inscriptions, fixed

as if on a tomb in time
& place, the past tense
   presents itself. Scrawled

in the Bar of Prima—*we*
men, friends
   forever, were here. Hostus,

our names, & Gaius. Goodbye. The baths,
when they burned, burned
   at midnight & no one

watched them or suffered. One
must imagine rather the spectacular
   fin de siècle swimming hall swallowed

in spindrift. The distant
edge of a city on the distant edge
   of an empire on fire.

Vestige

Sometime after it is over, both
of us shut in our months of silence, you say
there is for you one
final kindness I can render. You let
the claw-foot fill. I fold
your clothes on the countertop & watch
you lower your ass to the water. & when
it has softened the hard
marble-sized cyst there, I square
my thumbs & because I know
to show affection this way I press
down draining the milky fluid. To groom
its mate, you say, the Southeast
Asian macaque combs
each inch of fur
with its teeth. The cleaner fish, found
mostly on reefs in the Pacific, affixes
itself to its host & for half its life
survives on the other's dust. You thrust
your red backside skyward
with its cyst. This—feel—
is where the tail was once, as when,
in the dark crucible of the human, *homo
erectus* left the trees & traipsed
the paths of diaspora
toward the future. Followed

the horn of Africa. The pass
across the Strait & south
through California where you, also, walked
into my living room & whispered
it was finished. Followed
the Andes like a spine. You say
it is late. Like
it has always done the sun
is sliding again tonight to the Pacific. You lift
yourself to your feet & feel
behind you the nothing
I have left you, the vestige,
love, of what once
we were.

Scabies

I know them only—my almost
invisible bugs—by
    effect. Their empty, s-

shaped excavations snake
through my colonized skin. The sacs
    of their eggs flake first

from between my fingers then,
a day later, hang
    from the ends of my lashes. Eyeless

mite. Mouth. Louse
who beneath the lens resembles
    those creatures deep

in the galaxy we imagined ravaging
our future space-hopping progeny. Monster
    of skin. Mythic

sea serpent lurking
at the edges of sailors' maps. This means
    I am become myself the end

of the recognized world. I rub
the thin coat of Permethrin
    everywhere, my flesh—fit

climate for the tiny
beasts—greased. A Goldilocks
    zone astronomers call it. That district

of space capable,
as we are, of harboring
    life. My little

parasitical species. When we,
entomologists speculate, split
    from the ape scabies

followed. Evolved,
as we did, intricate
    forms for their hungry living. City

states. Chambers of larva
carved in the subcutaneous tissue.
    & when, pillaged

to its core, the warm world
rubs us out at last & ravenous
    still we lift

our eyes to the just right
ring of stars, scabies—faithful
    to the end—will be with us. At one time

they were all we could imagine
of love. In the mud
    we crawled from. In London

& Antwerp, the teeming
cities we split from—bug
    & man—for a land

of our own. Home,
here, in the far colonies
    of Europe. We burrowed

west. We had arrived,
we said, pregnant
    with faith.

Yosemite Lodge Food Court

Late in the season we eat
with plastic utensils our Western-
themed dinners. El Capitan
Tenders. Yosemite
Samburgers. The booth's
vinyl whines beneath us. My brother
lifts his face to the plate-
glass windows where,
in the last light of day, Half Dome—broken
capitol—flashes
then wanes. When,
in 1851, 200
Ahwahneechee retreated across the Valley,
a battalion of militia—Jim
Savage at its head—hunted
the natives to the very base
of the rock. The slaughter, story
has it, lasted
twenty minutes & for sixty days
stained the earth red. First
gold in Merced then,
by refrigerated railcar, corrals
of beef brought west
through mountain passes to fatten
the boomtown. Tonight,
the greatest generation grazes
its Taft Point Pasta. All

their lives they have worked for this, in
Bakersfield & Fresno sweated
at their machines to feel
at last, passing
beyond the city, the wind
in their chartered RVs. To see, sad
cow eyes rising to the window, what's
left. Next
to the bathhouse a herd of mule deer dozes
in Sentinel Meadow. At the edge
of the park, pine stands & scrub
brush burn. My brother,
I will miss you when it comes. When sometime
late in the Cenozoic, the smoking
earth turns
at last to the satisfaction
for which it has waited, the flames
from here to San Francisco licking
the planet clean of us clear
down to its plates of rock. Already
this fall, they are swallowing
the high timber. The tourists
wheel their tanks of oxygen
open. Slowly
we chew.

In a Year of Drought, I Drink Wine
in a Los Angeles Hot Tub

So too on Troy's final afternoon
the doomed children of the city sang. Such
   was their joy, Virgil tells us, such

was their simple awestruck wonder
at the great beast even
   the Achaeans, cramped, standing

on each other's shoulders inside
the close wood, wept. What
   he means, of course, is that inside

of the other's suffering, one
can imagine always aspects
   of some wild beauty refusing

negation. Or no. Not
that it exists, this
   beauty, but that

it can be made so. Rome,
Virgil says, springing
   from Ilion's ashes. Elsewhere

Orpheus. This
is not my home. Here
    for the weekend only, I float

out into the hot tub's bubbling, bleach-
& salt-scoured water. I watch
    the few stars the city permits

still flicker on, the long
avenues of light below them—Cienega
    & Sunset, Ventura—burn

& spangle in the mountains' dark bowl. The bottle
of vintage prosecco sweats. To secure
    for their desert metropolis water

enough to nourish all this, city
developers—circa
    the arrival, reports suggest, of something

like a hundred thousand drought-
struck families fleeing
    the plains' vast clouds of dust—drained

whole tracts of Valley farmland. The Los Angeles
River—wonder
 of brute, New Deal engineering—appeared

suddenly, punched
out from concrete & hope. & here
 at last the people drank. & maybe

it had to go wrong, that moment. Maybe
Troy's last carnival charms us,
 yes, because we know now how

the Achaeans came, who slayed
& cast from the walls of that city Astyanax,
 Hector's son. The swords, Virgil says,

were many & beautiful. Beyond
the lights of Wilshire Tower tonight, the dried-
 up & sewage-stuffed trench left

from that river rots. Not
one fountain in the city lifts,
 now, its mouth

of extravagant water skyward. Not
one far hill exists the flames have spared. Obscured
    in the smog & hot tub's steam, the sword

of Orion flashes. I fill
my glass to the rim. I raise it
    to the great hunter, that structure

of dust & flame flickering
above Los Angeles like a man—majestic, see,
    in his warrior's vestments—vanishing.

80 East, Nevada

              & in the opposite direction, west
from Omaha & Independence, the settlers
    of California traveled too
                    once, their wagons
            loaded with buckshot & sometimes
with dressers even & ovens along
      the same labyrinthine river, the Humboldt, the road
            still to this day trails. A day

out from San Francisco, we know
        the towns through which we pass—Nevada's
    sad, forgotten gold belt—by
        the massive hillside letters men
in those places arranged the rocks as. E
                   for Elko. O, there

    is always for us the hunger
to inscribe with our own narratives
        the wild, high-Sierra scrub of what
        we fear. To form,
as couples before us have done here, hearts
    of rock in the sand. Amanda
                & Jason. Nathan
& Sophia. Through such

a sentimental landscape our little
rented Penske passes. In back,
we have loaded what is mine
of the life we shared in California—
the folding chairs & floor lamps, the low
dependable bed on which
we too were a couple once. We,
who when it is over will begin
in our separate cities saying
we miss each other & what
is the weather like there & there
there. Then

is the highway a kind
of fuse too for us. Un-
settling. South

of this place, late one winter pinned
in the Wasatch Mountains, Margaret
Reed—her husband,
for killing a man, banished—begged
from William Graves for eight times
the going price a pair
of famished oxen. She watched
the children pick from their teeth even
the poor beasts' hooves & later, taking

care, she says, that no one
should consume a relative, they let
themselves at last imagine each other
as meat. We

understand now how
it is done. One
must loosen from the legbone whole
the hamstring. Strip
clean the deep fascia. That

was when, the histories say, Graves
came, the ache
of what he was owed low
in his gut & claimed
her debt in flesh. He fucked her
I mean. & we,

who have convinced ourselves
that when it is over even we
will talk, still, & be close, know
in our bitter, indigestible bones how barren
& uncrossable a continent
the heart is. How sheer
its cliffs. The cities

& towns along the highway here hand-

painted their geoglyphs red,
                              white, & blue in the wake
              of the towers' falling. We watch
              the C of Carlin, Nevada—flag-
colored outcropping—drop
                        away behind the Penske's insect-
speckled glass. We will pass
                        through many states still, you
                        & I, but we, we say,
          were in California once & young.

At My Sister's Wedding, I Dance the Dance of Swine

in German folk tradition, if an older sibling is unmarried by the time of his younger sibling's wedding, he is made to dance in a hog trough

In the country our kinfolk
came from, shame—ancientest
   of passions—had

still in the old years its uses. If you,
as I am, were, for instance, eldest
   of your family's siblings & if,

on the day of your sister's marriage, you remained
spouseless still, given
   rather to the Black Forest's fruitless

wastes & to brooding, you
danced also the hog's tarantella. The trough
   is wheeled to the floor. My father's

family, four
centuries in Ohio, lines
   the stage waiting

for the past's last
lingering ritual. My sister
   smiles. Her white

dress is everything
that I, imagining it, had imagined it
   would be & she, inside it,

is for the last time
the small & wiggling thing I held
   in the county hospital. Slop,

the trough means. That she
is the fairytale daughter gone
   tonight to some dark country of love

& dying & that I
am thirty & single. Still
   my family's name awaits

in me its future. My feet
work nimbly the mix
   of mud & wine. In Luke, Legion—demon

of many parts—plunges to the sea snared
in a herd of pigs. We played, Amy
   & I, wife

& husband in our mother's
kitchen. I admit
   it is the closest I have been

to living with a woman. Once,
in the old days, angered
   by the pride of humans, the brute gods

dropped among us one
of those chthonic monsters myth
    is abundant with. This

was a boar, the story explains, sated
only by the blood of children & if,
    as I was once, you

also were a man you mustered
with your people each autumn
    to slaughter over

& over the cloven-hoofed
hog. Our trough
    rocks beneath me. The mud, color

of shit, is sweeter
than you would believe. My people,
    who love me, are just.

Missed Connections

You were, one   post describes, flying   cross-country from

Boston. Blonde. Above   Las Vegas we made   eye contact & last

I saw you you   were in the terminal taken   by the crowd. How

precarious, love. With what   devoted vigilance we miss

each other as once,   the gods the bodies   of mortals made

their own momentarily.   Who pared   the skin & lived

among us un-   recognized. Did not,   we asked, the

very air   around us hum? The summer rose garden in Berkeley—

you were,   as turns a planet in the light, lifting   to your stare

an American   Beauty. You   with the glasses. The hat.

The heart   of artichoke loaded   in your basket who before

I could say hello rode   away. Oh stranger say   anything. Descend

as the gods beyond   the walls of Troy, the towers   at all

the gates blazing because   a man with a name   like a city missed   a woman. For this   the empire sliding   into ashes.

Disaster,   like love, is the stuff   of seconds. & yesterday—

our break-ups raging, our faces   kissing, squinched   up

like bats—passed   above us an asteroid the size of a city

block. A shot   across the bow is how   the TV described it,

inside,   even, the ring   of satellites circling

the planet. Passed   as once did not the rock   that killed

Dilophosaurus. Ships   in the night. The nineteen men we missed

that day   were from the beginning listed. We missed them

at Denver & San Diego. We were late   in Cleveland.   For each

drone death the President's   signature.   Menelaus—

For your face   I will send a thousand ships   & miss you.

We Are Made of Stardust & Will Explode

is the kind of thing I said then, desperate
for any woman I knew to let me
be, for her, that doomed beauty I believed
in still. It was the summer construction
stopped. Beyond the city the scaffolded
frames of half-finished mansions rose, bone-like
& empty, against the night while, inside
an abandoned Colonial open,
as yet, to the sky above it, I watched
with Leah Mackenzie the wheeling web
of light beginning to turn. Technically,
it is true. Inside the Big Bang the same
square millimeter of carbon became
both Pleiades & each small breast she let
fall to me in our dark bower. & we
were young in those days, yes, & staring up
we seemed at the bright center of some high
spectacular devastation claiming
everything. Stocks fell. Wars were on. Across
the suburbs the streets' scrollwork, zoned, we knew
for water & light, lay empty. Playgrounds
waited for their children. In fields, fire
hydrants blossomed. I wanted, romantic
that I was, that full stop astronomers
predict will happen someday. Disaster,
dictionaries say, meant misalignment
of the stars once I wanted that. Rather,

dawn came. Colors returned. Together
we dressed. *Desuetude*, Proust calls it, an object's
or person's long pedestrian descent
into ruin. Wiring stripped, the streetlights
of Foxglove Glen led us back. Above us,
the sunrise—rosy, we called it—clotted.

High School Graduation Party

They are all, of course, entirely too
cool to be here. They have learned exactly
that look of certain, self-assured contempt
they will wear this summer, bound, most of them,
for some lush campus somewhere their parents'
parents, dead now, never saw. For their small
dark rooms of Bacardi & sex. Envy
is not the word. Though I am old enough
now to understand there is no pleasure
more lasting than a Sunday afternoon
in Ohio, in the sunlight, with cake
& bunting, I admire, still, their studied
turning away. Who wouldn't? In a different
century, we would send them to war.

Death of the Star High School Running Back

Home this Christmas, the city
buried in snow, I approach
slowly the frozen fold of earth
where his parents laid him. There is
above his body not
the smallest suggestion of snow. No
skidding windblown foliage. Only
the flags of our people pulsing
on their tiny sticks. The swept
grass. We grow
the empire's dead devotedly
here in Ohio. On Fridays
I watched from the stands the man
he would become—cleated
like a man, made
to endure ruin
beautifully, like a man—march
untouched through the one-
hole to open
field. Even
then it was metaphor. Field
of Elysium. Field
of sand somewhere
in Saladin Province purpling
with blood. The bodies
of Imperial soldiers slaughtered—

9 A.D.—in the forests
of the Goths rotted
three winters til Rome, slowly
preparing its revenge, returned
& furious fed
the routed barbarians to their dogs. They dug
for their own avenged dead networks
of tombs in the hills & here,
while the woods of Germany burned, buried
what was left to them
of history. Here,
at the grave they have made
for him cleaner even
than the earth, they have worked
in advance their own names
on the stone. Sue,
his mother. Michael. Ryan, like
a child in bed between the two tucked. I touch
with numb fingers the chiseled
words. Purple
Heart. Bronze
Star. Son. It is sweet
& right. The sky
where he is waiting is grayer
than hell this winter. I watch
the shifting scuds of cloud close
above me like something

from a 19th century novel. Obvious
despair. Decline. Tonight,
in some far backwater
of the Republic, the son
of our god, swaddled
as one of us, will come
to save us. The nation
will praise him.

Pacific Standard

Against which, I mean, we
for the first time sounded
ourselves & were found
wanting. What
else could we do then but spread
to every corner we carved out
from sandstone & Sioux? *Sic.* It's
craved I meant, as Magellan,
who named the thing, sailing
around the Cape craved
home. The hushed
waters he thought
he saw, I see
nowhere tonight in the rising white-
capped combers off Pacifica. *Pax*
facere. To make, Magellan
believed, peaceful. To find
oneself at the edge
of the continent for the first time, as I
did at thirty, & to forget this
hour has happened almost everywhere. That men
for centuries scattered
their sicknesses before them like seed. That we,
who shadowed gold to the coast, confronted
only there a phenomenon beyond
our capacity for destruction. Something

like a violence utterly
other—the tumbling
scud. The sea-
stack & crag crumbling like what
do you know of power? How
can you not look away? Where
I am from, everyone
I know is asleep.

Acknowledgments

Many thanks to the editors of the following journals, in which versions of poems in this collection first appeared:

Arts.gov NEA Writers' Corner, Banango Street, Bat City Review, Best New Poets 2015, Connotation Press, Four Way Review, Gettysburg Review, Gulf Coast, Harpur Palate, Indiana Review, The Journal, Kenyon Review Online, Matter, Meridian, Narrative, The National Poetry Review, New Ohio Review, The New Republic, Ploughshares, Poetry Northwest, Southern Indiana Review, and *Upstart.*

This book owes an incalculable debt, as I do, to the many people from whose generosity it has benefited.

At John Carroll: To George Bilgere and Philip Metres, who showed me what a life in poetry could look like. And to Jake Oresick, the first of many poets I loathed and envied.

At Cornell: To Alice Fulton, Roger Gilbert, Phil Lorenz, Ken McClane, and Bob Morgan. To Michael Koch and Stephanie Vaughn, for opening their home to the writers at Cornell, and for making that program feel, in turn, just like a home. To Lyrae Van Clief-Stefanon, who read some of this work in its very earliest stages—and who was kind. To Sarah Scoles and Matt Grice, roommates far better than I deserved. To Allison Barrett, Ginger Heatter, Christopher Lirette, Elizabeth Lindsey Rogers, and Rebecca van Laer. To Justin Souza, for his keenest of criticism.

At Stanford: To Christina Ablaza, Eavan Boland, Simone Di Piero, Ken Fields, and Doug Powell. To my peers in the Stegner Program, from whom I learned much. To Kai Carlson-Wee, Lord of seventeen forever. To Mario Chard, Allison Davis, and Chiyuma Elliott. To Kimberly Grey, for my title, for her love. To Jon Hickey and Dana Koster. To Hugh Martin, for everything. To Rosalie Moffett and Matt Moser Miller. To Jacques Rancourt, whose advice on ordering this collection was instrumental. To Mira Rosenthal. To Solmaz Sharif, sparring partner extraordinaire. To Michael Shewmaker, Austin Smith, and Greg Wrenn. And to Corey Van Landingham—who read this manuscript more times than I can count and whose indefatigable criticism, encouragement, and love have made it—and me—far better. Thank you.

At large: To the National Endowment for the Arts, for its generous financial and artistic support. To Mary Broadway, Justin Carter, Tim DeMay, Terry Stewart, and Piper Wheeler. To Fred Solinger, in Jersey, sharing a dark corner of the American experiment. To Martha Collins, for believing in this book and for writing about it so generously. And to everyone at Four Way Books who helped make this book a reality, especially Sally Ball, Clarissa Long, Ryan Murphy, Emily Price, and Martha Rhodes, for whose vision and mentorship I am deeply grateful.

To Amy, Nicholas, Eric, Mom, and Dad.

And in memory of David Sanchez (II Marine Expeditionary Force) and Ryan Woodward (82nd Airborne), who died in Iraq in 2006 and 2007. *Relinquunt omnia servare rem publicam.*

Christopher Kempf has published poetry in *Best New Poets*, *The Gettysburg Review*, *The New Republic*, *PEN America*, and *Ploughshares*, among other places. Recipient of a National Endowment for the Arts Fellowship, as well as a Wallace Stegner Fellowship from Stanford University, he is the 2016-2017 Emerging Writer Lecturer at Gettysburg College and a Ph.D. candidate in English Literature at the University of Chicago. He received his MFA from Cornell University.

Publication of this book was made possible by grants and donations. We are also grateful to those individuals who participated in our 2016 Build a Book Program. They are:

Anonymous (8), Evan Archer, Sally Ball, Jan Bender-Zanoni, Zeke Berman, Kristina Bicher, Carol Blum, Lee Briccetti, Deirdre Brill, Anthony Cappo, Carla & Steven Carlson, Maxwell Dana, Machi Davis, Monica Ferrell, Martha Webster & Robert Fuentes, Dorothy Goldman, Lauri Grossman, Steven Haas, Mary Heilner, Henry Israeli, Christopher Kempf, David Lee, Jen Levitt, Howard Levy, Owen Lewis, Paul Lisicky, Katie Longofono, Cynthia Lowen, Louise Mathias, Nathan McClain, Gregory McDonald, Britt Melewski, Kamilah Moon, Carolyn Murdoch, Tracey Orick, Zachary Pace, Gregory Pardlo, Allyson Paty, Marcia & Chris Pelletiere, Eileen Pollack, Barbara Preminger, Kevin Prufer, Peter & Jill Schireson, Roni & Richard Schotter, Soraya Shalforoosh, Peggy Shinner, James Snyder & Krista Fragos, Megan Staffel, Marjorie & Lew Tesser, Susan Walton, Calvin Wei, Abigail Wender, Allison Benis White, and Monica Youn.